SENECA ON FRIENDSHIP, DEATH,
AND POVERTY
Part Three of *Seneca of a Happy Life*
by Roger L'Estrange ✖ Edited and Revised by Keith Seddon

Roger L'Estrange, staunch royalist, author and pamphleteer, one-time inmate of Newgate Prison, one-time exile, one-time Member of Parliament, takes up the teaching of the Roman Stoic philosopher Seneca, rearranging and paraphrasing the original Latin to shape a unique and engaging work of his own.

True friendship, based on Stoic principles, provides a certain antidote against all calamities, and even the fear of poverty, the hurt of death, and the lamentations of grief may be turned aside by those who possess a proper philosophy.

This third slim volume is the concluding part of Roger L'Estrange's *Seneca of a Happy Life*, being itself an extract of a much larger whole, *Seneca's Morals*, first published in 1678.

Keith Seddon is professor of philosophy at Warnborough College Ireland.

Roger L'Estrange's *Seneca of a Happy Life* (an extract from *Seneca's Morals By Way of Abstract: To which is added, A Discourse, under the Title of An After-Thought*), edited and revised by Keith Seddon, in Three Parts:

PART ONE
SENECA ON HAPPINESS, VIRTUE, AND
PHILOSOPHY AS THE GUIDE TO LIFE
[Chapters 1–7]

PART TWO
SENECA ON PROVIDENCE, MODERATION,
AND CONSTANCY OF MIND
[Chapters 8–16]

PART THREE
SENECA ON FRIENDSHIP, DEATH,
AND POVERTY
[Chapters 17–25]

OTHER BOOKS BY KEITH SEDDON:

Epictetus: The Discourses, Handbook and Fragments [forthcoming]
The Stoic Fragments of Epictetus [forthcoming]
An Outline of Cynic Philosophy: Antisthenes of Athens and Diogenes of Sinope in Diogenes Laertius Book Six (with C. D. Yonge)
A Summary of Stoic Philosophy: Zeno of Citium in Diogenes Laertius Book Seven (with C. D. Yonge)
Stoic Serenity: A Practical Course on Finding Inner Peace
Epictetus' Handbook and the Tablet of Cebes: Guides to Stoic Living
Lao Tzu: Tao Te Ching
Learning the Tao: Chuang Tzu as Teacher
Tractatus Philosophicus Tao: A short treatise on the Tao Te Ching of Lao Tzu
Time: A Philosophical Treatment

SENECA

ON FRIENDSHIP, DEATH,

AND POVERTY

�֍

Part Three

of

Seneca of a Happy Life

An Extract from

SENECA'S MORALS

by

Roger L'Estrange

Edited and Revised by Keith Seddon

LULU

Seneca of a Happy Life, part of *Seneca's Morals By way of Abstract: To which is added, A Discourse, under the Title of An After-Thought* by Roger L'Estrange, was first published in 1678.

This new edition first published 2011
by Lulu
www.lulu.com

Typeset in Bembo Book 12/15 pt

ISBN 978–1–4710–3581–4 (paperback)

Of all felicities, the most charming is that of a firm and gentle friendship. It sweetens all our cares, dispels our sorrows, and counsels us in all extremities.

CONTENTS

CHAPTER 17

OUR HAPPINESS DEPENDS IN A GREAT MEASURE UPON THE CHOICE OF OUR COMPANY

THE comfort of life depends upon conversation, good offices and concord; and human society is like the working of an arch of stone: all would fall to the ground if one piece did not support another. Above all things, let us have a tenderness for blood; and it is yet too little not to hurt, unless we profit one another. We are to relieve the distressed, to put the wanderer into his way, and to divide our bread with the hungry – which is but the doing of good to ourselves, for we are only several members of one great body. Nay, we are all of a consanguinity, formed of the same materials, and designed to the same end. This obliges us to a mutual tenderness and converse; and the other, to live with a regard to equity and justice. The love of society is natural, but the choice of our company is matter of virtue and prudence. Noble examples stir us up to noble actions, and the very history of large and public souls inspires a man with generous thoughts. It makes a man long to be in action, and doing of something that the world may be the better for; as protecting the weak, delivering the oppressed, punishing the insolent. It is a great blessing, the very conscience of giving a good example, beside that it is the greatest obligation any man can lay upon the age he lives in. He that converses with the proud shall be puffed up, a lustful acquaintance makes a man lascivious; and the way to secure a man from wickedness is to withdraw from the examples of it. It is too much to have them *near* us, but more to have them *within* us: ill examples, pleasure and ease, are, no doubt of it, great corrupters of manners. A rocky ground hardens the horses' hoof, the mountaineer makes the best soldier, the miner makes the best pioneer, and severity of discipline fortifies the mind. In all excesses and extremities of good, and of ill fortune, let us have recourse to great examples that have contemned both. *These are the best instructors that teach in their lives, and prove their words by their actions.*

AS an ill air may endanger a good constitution, so

Avoid even dissolute places, as well as loose companions

may a place of ill example endanger a good man. Nay, there are some places that have a kind of privilege to be licentious, and where luxury and dissolution of manners seem to be lawful; for great examples give both authority and excuse to wickedness. Those places are to be avoided as dangerous to our manners. *Hannibal* himself was unmanned by the looseness of *Campania*, and though a conqueror by his arms, he was overcome by his pleasures. I would as soon live among butchers as among cooks; not, but that a man may be temperate in any place, but, to see drunken men staggering up and down everywhere, and only the spectacles of lust, luxury and excess before our eyes, it is not safe to expose ourselves to the temptation. If the victorious *Hannibal* himself could not resist it, what shall become of us then that are subdued, and give ground to our lusts already? He that has to do with an enemy in his breast has a harder task upon him than he that is to encounter one in the field: his hazard is greater if he loses ground, and his duty is perpetual; for he has no place or time for rest. If I give way to pleasure, I must also yield to grief, to poverty, to labour, ambition, anger, until I am torn to pieces by my misfortunes and my lusts. But against all this, philosophy propounds a liberty, that is to say, a liberty from the service of accidents and fortune. There is not anything that does more mischief to mankind than mercenary masters of philosophy that do not live as they teach; they give a scandal to virtue. How can any man expect that a ship should steer a fortunate course, when the pilot lies wallowing in his own vomit? It is a usual thing, first to learn to do ill ourselves, and then to instruct others to do so. But that man must needs be very wicked, that has gathered into himself the wickedness of other people.

THE best conversation is with the philosophers, that is to say, with such of them as teach us matter, not words; that preach to us things necessary, and keep us to the *Practical philosophers are the best company* practice of them. There can be no peace in human life without the contempt of all events. There is nothing that either puts better thoughts into a man, or sooner sets him right that is out of the way, than a good companion. For the example has the force of a precept, and touches the heart with an affection to goodness. And not only the frequent hearing and seeing of a wise man delights us, but the very encounter of him suggests profitable contemplations, such as a man finds himself moved with when he goes into a holy place. I will take more care with *whom* I eat and drink, than *what*; for without a friend, the table is a manger. Writing does well, but personal discourse and conversation does better; for men give great credit to their ears, and take stronger impressions from example than precept. *Cleanthes* had never hit *Zeno* so to the life, if he had not been with him at all his privacies, if he had not watched and observed him, whether or not he practised as he taught. *Plato* got more from *Socrates'* manners than from his *words*; and it was not the *school*, but the *company* and *familiarity* of *Epicurus* that made *Metrodorus*, *Hermachus* and *Polyænus* so famous.

NOW, though it be by instinct that we covet society and avoid solitude, we should yet take *The more company the more danger* this along with us, that the more acquaintance the more danger. Nay, there is not one man of a hundred that is to be trusted with himself. If company cannot alter us, it may interrupt us; and he that so much as stops upon the way loses a great deal of a short life, which we yet make shorter by our inconstancy. If an enemy were at our heels, what haste should we make? But death is so, and yet we never mind it. There is no venturing of tender and easy natures among the people; for it is odds that they will go over to the major party. It would perhaps shake the constancy of *Socrates*, *Cato*, *Lælius*, or any of us all, even when our resolutions are at the height, to stand the shock of vice that presses upon us with a kind of public authority. It is a world of mischief that may be done by one single example of avarice or luxury. One voluptuous palate makes a great many more. A wealthy neighbour stirs up envy, and a fleering companion moves ill-nature wherever he comes. What will become of those people then, that expose themselves to a popular violence? – which is ill both ways, either if they comply with the wicked because they are many, or quarrel with the multitude because they are not principled alike. The best way is to retire, and associate only with those that may be the better for us, and we for them. These respects are mutual, for while we teach, we learn. To deal freely, I dare not trust myself in the hands of much company: I never go abroad, that I come home again the same man I went out. Something or other that I had put in order is discomposed: some passion that I had subdued gets head again, and it is just with our minds as it is after a long indisposition with our bodies; we are grown so tender that the least breath of air exposes us to a relapse. And it is no wonder if a numerous conversation be dangerous where there is scarce any single man, but by his discourse, example, or behaviour, does either recommend to us, or imprint in us, or by a kind of contagion, insensibly infect us with one vice or other; and the more people the greater is the peril. Especially let us have a care of public spectacles, where wickedness insinuates itself with pleasure; and above all others, let us avoid spectacles of cruelty and blood; and have nothing to do with those that are perpetually whining and complaining; there may be faith and kindness there, but no peace. People that are either sad or fearful, we do commonly, for their own sakes, set a guard upon them, for fear they should make an ill use of being alone: especially the imprudent, who are still contriving of mischief, either for others or for themselves, in cherishing their lusts, or forming their designs. So much for the choice of a *companion*; we shall now proceed to that of a *friend*.

CHAPTER 18

THE BLESSINGS OF FRIENDSHIP

OF all felicities, the most charming is that of a *firm* and *gentle friendship*. It sweetens all our cares, dispels our sorrows, and counsels us in all extremities. Nay, if there were no other comfort in it than the bare exercise of so generous a virtue, even for that single reason, a man would not be without it. Beside that, it is a sovereign antidote against all calamities, even against the fear of death itself.

BUT we are not yet to number our friends by the *visits* that are made us, and to confound *Every man is* the decencies of *ceremony* and *commerce* *not a friend that* with the offices of *united affections*. *Caius* *makes us a visit* *Graccus*, and after him *Livius Drusus*, were the men that introduced among the *Romans* the fashion of separating their visitants: some were taken into their *closet*, others were only admitted into the *antechamber*, and some again were fain to wait in the *hall* perhaps, or in the *court* – so that they had their *first*, their *second*, and their *third-rate* friends, but none of them true; only they are called so in course, as we salute strangers with some title or other of respect at a venture. There is no depending upon those men that only take their compliment in their turn, and rather slip through the door than enter at it: he will find himself in a great mistake that either seeks for a friend in a palace, or tries him at a feast.

THE great difficulty rests in the choice of him:
that is to say, in the first place, let him be
The choice of virtuous; for vice is contagious, and there
a friend is no trusting of the sound and the sick together. And he ought to be a wise man too, if a body
knew where to find him; but, in this case, he that is
least ill is best, and the highest degree of human prudence is only the most venial folly. That friendship,
where men's affections are cemented by an equal, and
by a common love of goodness, it is not either hope or
fear, or any private interest that can ever dissolve it,
but we carry it with us to our graves, and lay down
our lives for it with satisfaction. *Paulina's* good, and
mine (says our author) were so wrapped up together,
that in consulting her comfort, I provided for my
own: and when I could not prevail upon her to take
less care for me, she prevailed upon me to take more
care of myself. Some people make it a question,
whether it is the greater delight, the enjoying of an old
friendship, or the acquiring of a new one: but it is in
the preparing of a friendship, and in the possession of
it, as it is with a husbandman in sowing and reaping;
his delight is the hope of his labour in the one case, and
the fruit of it in the other. My conversation lies among
my books, but yet in the letters of a friend, methinks, I
have his company; and when I answer them, I do not
only write, but speak: and in effect, a friend is an eye, a
heart, a tongue, a hand, at all distances. When friends
see one another personally, they do not see one another as they do when they are divided, where the
meditation dignifies the prospect. But they are effec-

tually in a great measure absent, even when they are present. Consider their nights apart, their private studies, their separate employments and necessary visits, and they are almost as much together, divided, as present. True friends are the whole world to one another, and he that is a friend to himself is also a friend to mankind. Even in my very studies, the greatest delight I take in what I learn, is the teaching of it to others: for there is no relish, methinks, in the possessing of anything without a partner. Nay, if wisdom itself were offered me, upon condition only of keeping it to myself, I should undoubtedly refuse it.

LUCILIUS tells me that he was written to by a friend, but cautions me withal, not to say anything to him of the affair in question, for he himself stands upon the same guard. *There must be no reserves in friendship* What is this, but to affirm and to deny the same thing in the same breath; in calling a man a friend, whom we dare not trust as our own soul? For there must be no reserves in friendship: as much deliberation as you please before the league is struck, but no doubtings or jealousies after. It is a preposterous weakness to love a man before we know him, and not to care for him after. It requires time to consider of a friendship; but, the resolution once taken, entitles him to my very heart. I look upon my thoughts to be as safe in his breast as in my own; I shall, without any scruple, make him the confident of my most secret cares and counsels. It goes a great way toward the making of a man faithful, to let him understand that you think him so; and he that does but so much as suspect that I will

deceive him, gives me a kind of right to cozen him.
When I am with my friend, methinks I am alone, and
as much at liberty to speak anything as to think it; and,
as our hearts are one, so must be our interests and con-
venience: for friendship lays all things in common, and
nothing can be good to the one that is ill to the other. I
do not speak of such a community as to destroy one
another's propriety, but as the father and the mother
have two children, not one a-piece, but each of them
two.

    BUT, let us have a care above all things, that our
kindness be rightfully founded; for where
A generous
friendship
there is any other invitation to friendship
than the friendship itself, that friendship
will be bought and sold. He derogates from the majesty of it, that makes it only dependent upon good
fortune. It is a narrow consideration for a man to
please himself in the thought of a friend, because, says
he, *I shall have one to help me, when I am sick, in prison, or
in want.* A brave man should rather take delight in the
contemplation of doing the same offices for another.
He that loves a man for his own sake, is in an error. A
friendship of interest cannot last any longer than the
interest itself; and this is the reason that men in
prosperity are so much followed; and when a man
goes down the wind, nobody comes near him.
Temporary friends will never stand the test. One man
is forsaken for fear or profit, another is betrayed. It is a
negotiation, not a friendship, that has an eye to ad-
vantages: only through the corruption of times, that
which was formerly a friendship, is now become a

design upon a booty; alter your testament, and you lose your friend. But my end of friendship is to have one dearer to me than myself, and for the saving of whose life I would cheerfully lay down my own — taking this along with me, that only wise men can be friends; others are but companions: and that there is a great difference also betwixt love and friendship; the one may sometimes do us hurt, the other always does us good; for one friend is helpful to another in all cases, as well in prosperity as affliction. We receive comfort even at a distance, from those we love, but then it is light and faint: whereas presence and conversation touches us to the quick, especially if we find the man we love to be such a person as we wish.

IT is usual with princes to reproach the living, by commending the dead; and to praise *The loss of a* those people for speaking truth, from *friend is hardly* whom there is no longer any danger of *to be repaired* hearing it. This is *Augustus'* case. He was forced to banish his daughter *Julia* for her common and prostituted impudence; and still, upon fresh informations, he was often heard to say: *If* Agrippa *or* Mecænas *had been now alive, this would never have been.* But yet where the fault lay may be a question, for perchance it was his own, that had rather complain for the want of them, than seek for others as good. The *Roman* losses by war, and by fire, *Augustus* could quickly supply and repair; but for the loss of *two friends* he lamented his whole life after. *Xerxes* (a vain and foolish prince), when he made war upon *Greece*, one told him, *It would never come to a battle.* Another, *That he would find only empty cities and countries, for they would not so much as stand the very fame of his coming.* Others soothed him in the opinion of his *prodigious numbers*; and they all concurred to puff him up to his destruction. Only *Demaratus* advised him not to depend too much upon his numbers, for he would rather find them a burden to him than an advantage: and that three hundred men in the straits of the mountains would be sufficient to give a check to his whole army; and that such an accident would undoubtedly turn his vast numbers to his confusion. It fell out afterward as he foretold, and he had thanks for his fidelity. A miserable prince, that among so many thousand subjects, had but one servant to tell him the truth!

CHAPTER 19

HE THAT WOULD BE HAPPY MUST
TAKE AN ACCOUNT OF HIS TIME

IN the distribution of human life we find that a
great part of it passes away in *evil-doing*; a greater
yet in doing just *nothing at all*; and effectually the
whole, in doing things *beside our business*. Some hours
we bestow upon ceremony and servile attendances,
some upon our pleasures, and the remainder runs at
waste. What a deal of time is it that we spend in hopes
and fears, love and revenge; in balls, treats, making of
interests; suing for offices, soliciting of causes, and
slavish flatteries! The shortness of life, I know, is the
common complaint both of fools and philosophers, as
if the time we have were not sufficient for our duties.
But it is with our lives as with our estates, a good hus-
band makes a little go a great way; whereas, let the
revenue of a prince fall into the hand of a prodigal, it is
gone in a moment. So that the time allotted us, if it
were well employed, were abundantly enough to answer all the ends and purposes of mankind. But we
squander it away in avarice, drink, sleep, luxury,
ambition, fawning addresses, envy, rambling voyages,
impertinent studies, change of counsels, and the like;
and when our portion is spent, we find the want of it,
though we give no heed to it in the passage: insomuch,
that we have rather *made* our life short than *found* it so.
You shall have some people perpetually playing with
their fingers, whistling, humming, and talking to

themselves; and others consume their days in the composing, hearing, or reciting of songs and lampoons. How many precious mornings do we spend in consultation with barbers, tailors, and tire-women, patching and painting, betwixt the comb and the glass? A counsel must be called upon every hair we cut, and one curl amiss is as much as a body's life is worth. The truth is, we are more solicitous about our dress than our manners, and about the order of our periwigs, than that of the government. At this rate, let us but discount out of a life of a hundred years that time which has been spent upon popular negotiations, frivolous amours, domestic brawls, saunterings up and down to no purpose, diseases that we have brought upon ourselves, and this large extent of life will not amount perhaps to the minority of another man. It is a *long being*, but perchance a *short life*. And what is the reason of all this? We live as we should never die, and without any thoughts of human frailty, when yet the very moment we bestow upon this man, or thing, may peradventure be our last. But the greatest loss of time is delay and expectation, which depends upon the future. We let go the present, which we have in our own power, we look forward to that which depends upon fortune, and so quit a certainty for an uncertainty. We should do by time as we do by a torrent, make use of it while we may have it, for it will not last always.

THE calamities of human nature may be divided *No man can be happy,* into the *fear* of *death*, and the *miser-* *to whom life is irksome,* *ies* and *errors* of *life*. And it is the *or death terrible* great work of mankind to master the one and to rectify the other, and so to live, as neither to make life irksome to us, nor death terrible. It should be our care, before we are old, to live well, and when we are so, to die well, that we may expect our end without sadness; for it is the duty of life to prepare ourselves for death, and there is not an hour we live that does not mind us of our mortality: time runs on, and all things have their fate, though it lies in the dark. The period is certain to Nature, but what am I the better for it, if it be not so to me? We propound travels, arms, adventures, without ever considering that death lies in the way. Our time is set, and none of us know how near it is; but we are all of us agreed that the decree is unchangeable. Why should we wonder to have that befall us today, which might have happened to us any minute since we were born? Let us therefore live as if every moment were to be our last, and set our accounts right every day that passes over our heads. We are not ready for death, and therefore we fear it, because we do not know what will become of us when we are gone; and that consideration strikes us with an inexplicable terror. The way to avoid this distraction is to contract our business and our thoughts: when the mind is once settled, a day, or an age, is all one to us, and the series of time, which is now our trouble, will be then our delight. For he that is steadily resolved against all uncertainties shall never be disturbed with the variety of them. Let us make haste therefore to live, since every day to a wise man is a new life: for he has done his business the day before, and so prepared himself for the next, that if it be not his last, he knows yet that it might have been so. No man enjoys the true taste of life, but he that is willing and ready to quit it.

THE wit of man is not able to express the blindness of human folly in taking so much care of our fortunes, our houses, and our money, than we do of our lives; everybody breaks in upon the one *gratis*, but we betake ourselves to fire and sword if any man invades the other. There is no dividing in the case of patrimony, but people share our time with us at pleasure: so profuse are we of that only thing whereof we may be honestly covetous. It is a common practice to ask an hour or two of a friend for such or such a business, and it is as easily granted; both parties only considering the occasion, and not the thing itself. They never put time to account, which is the most valuable of all precious things: but because they do not see it, they reckon upon it as nothing, and yet these easy men, when they come to die, would give the whole world for those hours again, which they so inconsiderately cast away before; but there is no recovering of them. If they could number their days that are yet to come, as they can those that are already past, how would those very people tremble at the apprehension of death, though a hundred years hence, that never so much as think of it at present, though they know not but it may take them away the next immediate minute? It is a usual saying, *I would give my life for such or such a friend*, when at the same time we do give it without so much as thinking of it: nay, when that friend is never the better for it, and we ourselves the worse. Our time is set, and

We take more care of our fortunes, than of our lives

day and night we travel on: there is no baiting by the way, and it is not in the power of either prince or people to prolong it. Such is the love of life that even those decrepit dotards that have lost the use of it will yet beg the continuance of it, and make themselves younger than they are, as if they could cozen even fate itself. When they fall sick, what promises of amendment if they escape that bout: what exclamations against the folly of their misspent time? And yet, if they recover, they relapse. No man takes care to live well, but long; when it is yet in everybody's power to do the former, and in no man's to do the latter. We consume our lives in providing the very instruments of life, and govern ourselves still with a regard to the future, so that we do not properly live, but we are about to live. How great a shame is it, to be laying new foundations of life at our last gasp, and for an old man (that can only prove his age by his beard) with one foot in the grave, to go to school again? While we are young, we may learn: our minds are tractable, and our bodies fit for labour and study, but when age comes on, we are seized with languor and sloth, afflicted with diseases, and at last we leave the world as ignorant as we come into it: only we *die* worse than we were *born*, which is none of Nature's fault, but ours; for our fears, suspicions, perfidy, &c. are from ourselves. I wish with all my soul that I had thought of my end sooner, but I must make the more haste now, and spur on, like those that set out late upon a journey; it will be better to learn late than not at all, though it be only to instruct me how I may leave the stage with honour.

IN the division of life, there is time *present, past,* and *to come.* What we *do,* is *short;* what we shall do, is *doubtful;* but what we *have done,* is *certain,* and out of the power of fortune. The passage of time is wonderfully quick, and a man must look backward to see it: and in that retrospect, he has all past ages at a view. But the present gives us the slip unperceived. It is but a moment that we live, and yet we are dividing it into *childhood, youth, man's estate,* and *old age,* all which degrees we bring into that narrow compass. If we do not watch, we lose our opportunities; if we do not make haste, we are left behind; our best hours escape us, the worst are to come. The purest part of our life runs first, and leaves only the dregs at the bottom; and *that time, which is good for nothing else, we dedicate to virtue*; and only propound to begin to live at an age that very few people arrive at. What greater folly can there be in the world than this loss of time, the future being so uncertain, and the damages so irreparable? If death be necessary, why should any man fear it? And if the time of it be uncertain, why should not we always expect it? We should therefore first prepare ourselves by a virtuous life, against the dread of an inevitable death. And it is not for us to put off being good until such or such a business is over: for one business draws on another, and we do as good as sow it; one grain produces more. It is not enough to philosophise when we have nothing else to do; but we must attend wisdom, even to the

Time present, past, and to come

neglect of all things else, for we are so far from having time to spare, that the age of the world would be yet too narrow for our business; nor is it sufficient not to omit it, but we must not so much as intermit it.

THERE is nothing that we can properly call our own, but our time, and yet everybody fools us out of it, that has a mind to it. If a man borrows a paltry sum of money, there must be bonds and securities, and every *We can call nothing our own, but our time* common civility is presently charged upon account: but he that has my time thinks he owes me nothing for it, though it be a debt that gratitude itself can never repay. I cannot call any man poor that has enough still left, be it never so little: it is good advice yet to those that have the world before them, to play the good husbands betimes, for it is too late to spare at the bottom, when all is drawn out to the lees. He that takes away a day from me, takes away what he can never restore me. But our time is either *forced away* from us, or *stolen* from us, or *lost*: of which the last is the foulest miscarriage. It is in life as in a journey: a book, or a companion, brings us to our lodging before we thought we were half way. Upon the whole matter we consume ourselves one upon another, without any regard at all to our own particular. I do not speak of such as live in notorious scandal, but even those men themselves, whom the world pronounces happy, are smothered in their felicities; servants to their professions and clients, and drowned in their lusts. We are apt to complain of the haughtiness of *great men*, when yet there is hardly any of them all so proud, but that at some time or other a man may yet have access to him, and perhaps a good word or look into the bargain. Why do we not rather complain of *ourselves*, for being of all others, even to ourselves, the most deaf and inaccessible?

COMPANY and business are great devourers of time, and our vices destroy our lives as well as our fortunes. The present is but a moment, and perpetually in flux; the time past we call to mind when we please, and it will abide the examination and inspection. But the busy man has not leisure to look back, or if he has, it is an unpleasant thing to reflect upon a life to be repented of: whereas the conscience of a good life puts a man into a secure and perpetual possession of a felicity never to be disturbed or taken away. But he that has led a wicked life is afraid of his own memory, and in the review of himself he finds only appetite, avarice or ambition, instead of virtue. But still he that is not at leisure many times to live, must, when his fate comes, whether he will or no, be at leisure to die. Alas! What is time to eternity? The age of a man to the age of the world? And how much of this little do we spend in fears, anxieties, tears, childhood! Nay, we sleep away the one half. How great a part of it runs away in luxury and excess, the ranging of our guests, our servants, and our dishes? As if we were to eat and drink not for satiety, but ambition. The nights may well seem short that are so dear bought, and bestowed upon wine and women. The day is lost in expectation of the night, and the night in the apprehension of the morning.

Company and business are great devourers of time

There is a terror in our very pleasures, and this vexa-
tious thought in the very height of them, that *they will
not last always*: which is a canker in the delights even of
the greatest and the most fortunate of men.

CHAPTER 20

HAPPY IS THE MAN WHO MAY CHOOSE HIS OWN BUSINESS

O H! The blessings of privacy and leisure! The wish of the powerful and eminent, but the privilege only of inferiors, who are the only people that live to themselves: nay, the very thought and hope of it is a consolation, even in the middle of all the tumults and hazards that attend greatness. It was *Augustus'* prayer that he might live to retire, and deliver himself from public business. His discourses were still pointing that way, and the highest felicity which this mighty prince had in prospect was the divesting himself of that illustrious state, which, how glorious soever in show, had at the bottom of it only anxiety and care. But it is one thing to retire for pleasure and another thing for virtue; which must be active, even in that retreat, and give proof of what it has learned: for a good and a wise man does in privacy consult the well-being of posterity. *Zeno* and *Chrysippus* did greater things in their studies than if they had led armies, borne offices, or given laws; which in truth they did, not to one city alone, but to all mankind: their quiet contributed more to the common benefit than the *sweat* and *labour* of other people. That retreat is not worth the while, which does not afford a man greater and nobler work than business. There is no slavish attendance upon great officers, no canvassing for places, no making of parties, no disappointments in my pretension to this charge, to that regiment, or to such or such a title; no envy of any man's favour or fortune, but a calm enjoyment of the general bounties of Providence, in company with a good conscience. A wise man is never so busy as in the solitary contemplation of God and the works of Nature. He withdraws himself to attend the service of future ages. And those counsels which he finds salutary to himself, he commits to writing for the good of after-times, as we do the receipts of sovereign antidotes, or balsams. He that is well employed in his study, though he may seem to do nothing at all, does the greatest things yet of all others, in affairs both human and divine. To supply a friend with a sum of money, or give my voice for an office, these are only private and particular obligations; but he that lays down precepts for the governing of our lives and the moderating of our passions, obliges human nature, not only in the present, but in all succeeding generations.

HE that would be quiet, let him repair to his philosophy, a study that has credit with all sorts of men. The eloquence of the bar, or whatsoever else addresses to the people, is *Philosophy is a quiet study* never without enemies: but philosophy minds its own business, and even the worst have an esteem for it. There can never be such a conspiracy against virtue; the world can never be so wicked, but the very name of a *philosopher* shall still continue venerable and sacred. And yet philosophy itself must be handled modestly, and with caution. But what shall we say of *Cato* then, for his meddling in the broil of a civil war, and interposing himself in the quarrel betwixt two enraged princes? He, that when *Rome* was split into *two factions*, between *Pompey* and *Cæsar*, declared himself against *both*. I speak this of *Cato's* last part, for in his former time the commonwealth was made unfit for a wise man's administration. All he could do then, was but bawling and beating of the air: one while he was lugged and tumbled by the rabble, spit upon, and dragged out of the *forum*, and then again hurried out of the senate-house to prison. There are some things which we propound originally, and others that fall in as accessary to another proposition. If a wise man retire, it is no matter whether he does it because the commonwealth was wanting to him, or because he was wanting to it. But to what republic shall a man betake himself? Not to *Athens*, where *Socrates* was condemned, and whence *Aristotle* fled for fear he should have been condemned too, and where virtue was oppressed by envy. Not to *Carthage*, where there was nothing but tyranny, injustice, cruelty and ingratitude. There is scarce any government to be found that will either endure a wise man, or which a wise man will endure: so that privacy is made necessary, because the only thing which is better is nowhere to be had. A man may commend navigation, and yet caution us against those seas that are troublesome and dangerous: so that he does as good as command me not to weigh anchor, that commends sailing only upon these terms. He that is a slave to business, is the most wretched of slaves.

CHOOSING OUR OWN BUSINESS

BUT how shall I get myself at liberty? We can run any
hazards for money, take any pains for hon-   *Liberty is to*
our, and why do we not venture something   *be purchased*
also for leisure and freedom? – without   *at any rate*
which we must expect to live and die in a tumult. For
so long as we live in public, business breaks in upon us,
as one billow drives on another, and there is no avoid-
ing it with either modesty or quiet. It is a kind of
whirlpool that sucks a man in, and he can never disen-
gage himself. A man of business cannot in truth be said
to live, and not one of a thousand understands how to
do it: for how to live and how to die, is the lesson of
every moment of our lives. All other arts have their
masters. As a busy life is always a miserable life, so is it
the greatest of all miseries to be perpetually employed
upon *other people's business*; for to sleep, to eat, to drink
at their hours, to walk their pace, and to love and hate
as they do, is the vilest of servitudes. Now though
business must be quitted, let it not be done unseasona-
bly; the longer we defer it, the more we endanger our
liberty; and yet we must no more fly before the time
than linger when the time comes, or however, we
must not love business for business sake; nor indeed do
we, but for the profit that goes along with it: for we
love the reward of misery, though we hate the misery
itself. Many people, I know, seek business without
choosing it, and they are even weary of their lives
without it, for want of entertainment in their own
thoughts. The hours are long and hateful to them
when they are alone, and they seem as short on the
other side in their debauches. When they are no longer

candidates, they are *suffragants*. When they give over other people's business, they do their own; and pretend business, but they make it, and value themselves upon being thought men of employment. Liberty is the thing which they are perpetually a-wishing, and never come to obtain, a thing neither to be bought nor sold; but a man must ask it of himself, and give it to himself. He that has given proof of his virtue in public, should do well to make trial of it in private also. It is not that solitude or a country life teaches innocence or frugality, but vice falls of itself, without witnesses and spectators; for the thing it designs is to be taken notice of. Did ever any man put on rich clothes not to be seen? Or spread the pomp of his luxury where nobody was to take notice of it? If it were not for admirers and spectators, there would be no temptations to excess; the very keeping of us from exposing them cures us of desiring them, for vanity and intemperance are fed with ostentation.

HE that has lived at sea in a storm, let him retire *Several people* and die in the haven; but let his retreat be *withdraw for* without ostentation, and wherein he may *several ends* enjoy himself with a good conscience, without the want, the fear, the hatred, or the desire of anything: not out of a malevolent detestation of mankind, but for satisfaction and repose. He that shuns both business and men, either out of envy, or any other discontent, his retreat is but to the life of a mole: nor does he live to himself, as a wise man does, but to his bed, his belly, and his lusts. Many people seem to retire out of a weariness of public affairs and the trouble of disappointments; and yet ambition finds them out even in that recess, into which fear and weariness had cast them; and so does luxury, pride, and most of the distempers of a public life. There are many that lie close, not that they may live securely, but that they may transgress more privately. It is their conscience, not their states that make them keep a porter, for they live at such a rate that to be seen before they be aware, is to be detected. *Crates* saw a young man walking by himself: *Have a care*, says he, *of lewd company*. Some men are busy in idleness, and make peace more laborious and troublesome than war: nay, and more wicked too, when they bestow it upon such lusts and other vices, which even the licence of a military life would not endure. We cannot call these people men of leisure, that are wholly taken up with their pleasures. A troublesome life is much to be preferred before a slothful one; and it is a strange thing, methinks, that any man should fear death, that has buried himself alive; as privacy, without letters, is but the burying of a man quick.

THERE are some that make a boast of their retreat, which is but a kind of lazy ambition. *Some men* They retire to make people talk of them, *retire to be* whereas I would rather withdraw to speak *talked of* with myself. And what shall that be, but that which we are apt to speak of one another? I will speak ill of myself, I will examine, accuse, and punish my infirmities. I have no design to be cried up for a great man, that has renounced the world in a contempt of the vanity and madness of human life; I blame nobody but myself, and I address only to myself. He that comes to me for help is mistaken, for I am not a physician, but a patient. And I shall be well enough content to have it said, when any man leaves me, *I took him for a happy and a learned man, and truly I find no such matter.* I had rather have my retreat pardoned than envied. There are some creatures that confound their footing about their dens, that they may not be found out, and so should a wise man in the case of his retirement. When the door is open, the thief passes it by, as not worth his while; but when it is bolted and sealed, it is a temptation for people to be prying. To have it said *that such a one is never out of his study, and sees nobody, &c.* this furnishes matter for discourse. He that makes his retirement too strict and severe does as good as call company to take notice of it.

EVERY man knows his own constitution. One *Philosophy re-* eases his stomach by vomit, another sup- *quires privacy,* ports it with good nourishment; he that *and freedom* has the gout forbears wine and bathing, and every man applies to the part that is most infirm. He that shows a gouty foot, a lame hand, or contracted nerves, shall be permitted to lie still and attend his cure. And why not so in the vices of his mind ? We must discharge all impediments and make way for philosophy, as a study inconsistent with common business. To all other things we must deny ourselves openly and frankly. When we are sick we refuse visits, keep ourselves close, and lay aside all public cares; and shall we not do as much when we philosophise? Business is the drudgery of the world, and only fit for

36

slaves, but contemplation is the work of wise men. Not but that solitude and company may be allowed to take their turns: the one creates in us the love of mankind, the other that of ourselves. Solitude relieves us when we are sick of company, and conversation when we are weary of being alone, so that the one cures the other. *There is no man*, in fine, *so miserable, as he that is at a loss how to spend his time*. He is restless in his thoughts, unsteady in his counsels, dissatisfied with the present, solicitous for the future; whereas he that prudently computes his hours and his business, does not only fortify himself against the common accidents of life, but improves the most rigorous dispensations of Providence to his comfort, and stands firm under all the trials of human weakness.

CHAPTER 21

THE CONTEMPT OF DEATH MAKES ALL MISERIES OF LIFE EASY TO US

I T is a hard task to master the natural desire of life by a philosophical contempt of death, and to convince the world that there is no hurt in it, and crush an opinion that was brought up with us from our cradles. What help? What encouragement? What shall we say to human frailty, to carry it fearless through the fury of flames and upon the points of swords? What rhetoric shall we use to bear down the universal consent of people to so dangerous an error? The captious and superfine subtleties of the schools will never do the work: these speak many things sharp, but utterly unnecessary, and void of effect. The truth of it is, there is but one chain that holds all the world in bondage, and that is the love of life. It is not that I propound the making of death so indifferent to us, as it is whether a man's hairs be even or odd: for what with self-love, and an implanted desire in everything of preserving itself, and a long acquaintance betwixt the soul and body, friends may be loath to part, and death may carry an appearance of evil, though in truth it is itself no evil at all. Beside that, we are to go to a strange place, in the dark, and under great uncertainties of our future state; so that people die in terror, because they do not know whither they are to go, and they are apt to fancy the worst of what they do not

38

understand: these thoughts are indeed sufficient to startle a man of great resolution, without a wonderful support from above. And moreover, our natural scruples and infirmities are assisted by the wits and fancies of all ages, in their infamous and horrid description of another world: nay, taking it for granted that there will be no reward and punishment, they are yet more afraid of annihilation than of hell itself.

BUT what is it we fear? *Oh! It is a terrible thing to die.* Well! And is it not better once to suffer it, than always to fear it? The earth itself *It is a folly to fear death* suffers both *with* me, and *before* me. How many islands are swallowed up in the sea? How many towns do we sail over? Nay, how many nations are wholly lost, either by inundations, or earthquakes? And shall I be afraid of my little body? Why should I, that am sure to die, and that all other things are mortal, be fearful of coming to my last gasp myself? It is the fear of death that makes us base, and troubles and destroys the life that we would preserve, that aggravates all circumstances, and makes them formidable. We depend but upon a flying moment. Die we must, but when? What is that to us? It is the law of Nature, the tribute of mortals, and the remedy of all evils. It is only the disguise that affrights us, as children that are terrified with a vizor. Take away the instruments of death, the fire, the axe, the guards, the executioners, the whips and the racks, take away the pomp, I say, and the circumstances that accompany it, and death is no more than what my slave yesterday contemned. The pain is nothing to a fit of the stone: if it be tolerable, it is not great; and if intolerable, it cannot last long. There is nothing that Nature has made necessary which is more easy than death: we are longer a-coming into the world than going out of it; and there is not any minute of our lives wherein we may not reasonably expect it. Nay, it is but a moment's work, the parting of the soul and body. What a shame is it then to stand in fear of anything so long, that is over so soon?

NOR is it any great matter to overcome this fear, *The fear of* for we have examples, as well of the *mean-* *death is easily* *est* of men, as of the *greatest* that have done *overcome* it. There was a fellow to be exposed upon the theatre, who in disdain, thrust a stick down his own throat, and choked himself; and another on the same occasion, pretending to nod upon the chariot, as if he were asleep, cast his head betwixt the spokes of the wheel, and kept his seat until his neck was broken. *Caligula,* upon a dispute with *Canius Julius: Do not flatter yourself,* says he, *for I have given order to put you to death. —I thank your most gracious majesty for it,* says *Canius,* giving to understand, perhaps, that, under his government, death was a mercy: for he knew that *Caligula* seldom failed of being as good as his word in that case. He was at play when the officer carried him away to his execution, and beckoning to the centurion, *Pray,* says he, *will you bear me witness, when I am dead and gone, that I had the better of the game.* He was a man exceedingly beloved and lamented, and for a farewell, after he had preached moderation to his friends: *You,* says he, *are here disputing about the immortality of the soul, and I am now going to learn the truth of it; if I discover anything upon that point, you shall hear of it.* Nay, the most timorous of creatures, when they see there is no escaping, they oppose themselves to all dangers; the despair gives them courage, and the necessity overcomes the fear. *Socrates* was thirty days in prison after his sentence, and had time enough to have starved himself, and so to have prevented the poison; but he gave the world the blessing of his life as long as he could, and took that fatal draught in the meditation and contempt of death. *Marcellinus*, in a deliberation upon death, called several of his friends about him: one was fearful, and advised what he himself would have done in the case; another gave the counsel which he thought *Marcellinus* would like best; but a friend of his, that was a *Stoic* and a stout man, reasoned the matter to him after this manner: *Marcellinus*, do not trouble yourself, as if it were such a mighty business that you have now in hand; it is nothing to *live*; all your servants do it, nay, your very beasts too; but to *die* honestly and resolutely, that is a great point. Consider with yourself, there is nothing pleasant in life, but what you have tasted already, and that which is to come is but the same thing over again; and how many men are there in the world that rather choose to die than to suffer the nauseous tediousness of the repetition? Upon which discourse he fasted himself to death. It was the custom of *Pacuvius* to solemnise in a kind of pageantry, every day, his own funeral. When he had swilled and gormandised to a luxurious and beastly excess, he was carried away from supper to bed, with this song and acclamation, *He has lived, he has lived.* That which he did in lewdness would become us to do in sobriety and prudence. If it shall please God to add another day to our lives, let us thankfully receive it; but however, it is our happiest and securest course, so to compose ourselves tonight, that we may have no anxious dependence upon tomorrow. *He that can say, I have lived this day, makes the next clear again.*

DEATH is the worst that either the severity of the *He that despises death, fears nothing* laws or the cruelty of tyrants can impose upon us, and it is the utmost extent of the dominion of fortune. He that is fortified against that, must consequently be superior to all other difficulties that are but in the way to it. Nay, and on some occasions, it requires more courage to live than to die. He that is not prepared for death shall be perpetually troubled, as well with vain apprehensions as with real dangers. It is not death itself that is dreadful, but the fear of it that goes before it. When the mind is under a consternation, there is no state of life that can please us; for we do not so much endeavour to avoid mischiefs, as to run away from them: and the greatest slaughter is upon a flying enemy. Had not a man better breathe out his last once and for all, than lie agonising in pains, consuming by inches, losing of his blood by drops; and yet, how many are there that are ready to betray their country and their friends, and to prostitute their very wives and daughters, to preserve a miserable carcass? Madmen and children have no apprehension of death, and it were a shame that our reason should not do as much toward our security as their folly. But, the great matter is to die considerately and cheerfully upon the foundation of virtue, for life, in itself, is irksome, and only eating and drinking in a circle.

HOW many are there, that betwixt the apprehensions of death and the miseries of life, are at their wits end what to do with themselves? *All men must die* Wherefore let us fortify ourselves against those calamities, from which the prince is no more exempt than the beggar. *Pompey* the Great had his head taken off by a boy, and a eunuch (young *Ptolemy* and *Photinus*). *Caligula* commanded the tribune *Dæcimus* to kill *Lepidus*; and another tribune (*Chæreus*) did as much for *Caligula*. Never was any man so great, but he was as liable to suffer mischief, as he was able to do it. Has not a thief, or an enemy, your throat at his mercy? Nay, and the meanest of servants has the power of life and death over his master, for whosoever contemns his own life, may be the master of another body's. You will find in history that the displeasure of servants has been as fatal as that of tyrants: and what matters it, the power of him we fear, when the thing we fear is in everybody's power? Suppose I fall into the hands of an enemy, and the conqueror condemns me to be led in triumph: it is but carrying me thither, whither I should have gone without him; that is to say, toward death, whither I have been marching ever since I was born. It is the fear of our last hour that disquiets all the rest. By the justice of all constitutions, mankind is condemned to a capital punishment: now, how despicable would that man appear, who being sentenced to death

in common with the whole world, should only peti-
tion that he might be the last man brought to the
block? Some men are particularly afraid of thunder,
and yet extremely careless of other, and of greater
dangers, as if that were all they have to fear. Will not a
sword, a stone, a fever, do the work as well? Suppose
the bolt should hit us, it were yet braver to die with a
stroke than with the bare apprehension of it, beside the
vanity of imagining that heaven and earth should be
put into such a disorder only for the death of one man.
A good and a brave man is not moved with lightning,
tempest, or earthquakes: but perhaps he would volun-
tarily plunge himself into that gulf, where otherwise
he should only fall; the cutting of a corn, or the swal-
lowing of a fly, is enough to dispatch a man; and it is
no matter how great that is, that brings me to my
death, so long as death itself is but little. Life is a small
matter, but it is a matter of importance to contemn it.
Nature that begat us, expels us, and a better and a safer
place is provided for us. And what is death, but a ceas-
ing to be what we were before? We are kindled, and
put out: to cease to be, and not to begin to be, is the
same thing. We die daily, and while we are growing,
our life decreases. Every moment that passes takes
away part of it; all that is past is lost: nay, we divide
with death the very instant that we live. As the last
sand in the glass does not measure the hour, but fin-
ishes it, so the last moment that we live does not make
up death, but concludes. There are some that pray
more earnestly for death than we do for life, but it is

better to receive it cheerfully when it comes, than to hasten it before the time.

BUT what is it that we would live any longer for? Not for our pleasures, for those we have tasted over and over, even to satiety: so that there is no point of luxury that is new to us. *But a man would be loath to leave his country and his friends behind him.* That is to say, he would have them go first, for that is the least part of his care. *Well! But I would fain live to do more good, and discharge myself in the offices of life*: as if to die were not the duty of every man that lives. We are loath to leave our possessions, and no man swims well with his luggage. We are all of us equally fearful of death and ignorant of life, but what can be more shameful than to be solicitous upon the brink of security? If death be at any time to be feared, it is always to be feared; but the way never to fear it, is to be often thinking of it. To what end is it to put off, for a little while, that which we cannot avoid? He that dies, does but follow him that is dead. *Why are we then so long afraid of that which is so little a while a doing?* How miserable are those people that spend their lives in the dismal apprehensions of death! For they are beset on all hands, and every minute in dread of a surprise. We must therefore look about us, as if we were in an enemy's country, and consider our last hour, not as a punishment, but as the law of Nature. The fear of it is a continual palpitation of the heart, and he that overcomes that terror shall never be troubled with any other. Life is a navigation; we are perpetually wallowing and dashing one against another; sometimes we

To what end should we covet life?

45

suffer shipwreck, but we are always in danger, and in expectation of it. And what is it when it comes, but either the end of a journey, or a passage? It is as great a folly to fear *death*, as to fear *old age*; nay, as to fear *life* itself, for he that would not die ought not to live, since death is the condition of life. Beside that, it is a madness to fear a thing that is certain, for where there is no doubt, there is no place for fear.

W E are still chiding of fate, and even those that exact the most rigorous justice betwixt man and man, are yet themselves unjust to Providence. *Why was such a one taken away in the prime of his years?* As if it were the number of years that makes death easy to us, and not the temper of the mind. He that would live a little longer today, would be as loath to die a hundred years hence. But which is more reasonable, for us to obey Nature, or for Nature to obey us? Go we must at last, and no matter how soon. It is the work of fate to make us live long, but it is the business of virtue to make a short life sufficient. Life is to be measured by action, not by time; a man may die old at thirty, and young at fourscore. Nay, the one lives after death, and the other perished before he died. I look upon age among the effects of chance. How long I shall live is in the power of others, but it is in my own, how well. The largest space of time is to live until a man is wise. He that dies of old age does no more than go to bed when he is weary. Death is the test of life, and it is that only which discovers what we are, and distinguishes betwixt ostentation and virtue. A man may dispute, cite

To die, is to obey Nature

46

great authorities, talk learnedly, huff it out, and yet be rotten at heart. But let us soberly attend our business, and since it is uncertain *when* or *where* we shall die, let us look for death in all places, and at all times. We can never study that point too much, which we can never come to experiment, whether we know it or no. It is a blessed thing to dispatch the business of life before we die, and then to expect death in the possession of a happy life. He is the great man, that is willing to die when his life is pleasant to him. An honest life is not a greater good than an honest death. How many brave young men, by an instinct of nature, are carried on to great actions, and even to the contempt of all hazards?

IT is childish to go out of the world groaning and wailing, as we came into it. Our bodies *It is childish* must be thrown away, as the secundine *to die* that wraps up the infant, the other being *lamenting* only the covering of the soul. We shall then discover the secrets of Nature; the darkness shall be discussed, and our souls irradiated with light and glory: a glory without a shadow, a glory that shall surround us, and from whence we shall look down and see day and night beneath us. If we cannot lift up our eyes toward the lamp of heaven without dazzling, what shall we do when we come to behold the divine light in its illustrious original? That death which we so much dread and decline, is not a determination, but the intermission of a life which will return again. All those things that are the very cause of life, are the way to death: we fear it, as we do fame, but it is a great folly to fear words. Some people are so impatient of life that they are still wishing for death; but he that wishes to die, does not desire it; let us rather wait God's pleasure, and pray for health and life. If we have a mind to live, why do we wish to die? If we have a mind to die, we may do it without talking of it. Men are a great deal more resolute in the article of *death* itself, than they are about the circumstances of it. For it gives a man courage to consider that his fate is inevitable; the slow approaches of death are the most troublesome to us, as we see many a gladiator who, upon his wounds, will direct his adversary's weapon to his very heart, though but timorous perhaps in the combat. There are some that have not the heart either to live or die; that is a sad case. But this we are sure of: *The fear of death is a continual slavery, as the contempt of it is certain liberty.*

CHAPTER 22

CONSOLATIONS AGAINST DEATH, FROM THE PROVIDENCE AND THE NECESSITY OF IT

THIS life is only a prelude to eternity, where we are to expect another original, and another state of things. We have no prospect of heaven here, but at a distance; let us therefore expect our last and decretory hour with courage. The last, I say, to our bodies, but not to our minds: our luggage we must leave behind us, and return as naked out of the world as we came into it. The day which we fear as our last is but the birthday of our eternity, and it is the only way to it: so that what we fear as a rock, proves to be but a port, in many cases to be desired, never to be refused, and he that dies young has only made a quick voyage of it. Some are becalmed, others cut it away before the wind, and we live just as we sail: first, we run our childhood out of sight, our youth next, and then our middle age: after that follows old age, and brings us to the common end of mankind. It is a great Providence that we have more ways out of the world than we have into it. Our security stands upon a point, the very article of death. It draws a great many blessings into a very narrow compass, and although the fruit of it does not seem to extend to the defunct, yet the difficulty of it is more than balanced by the contemplation of the future. Nay, suppose that all the business of this world should be forgotten, or my memory traduced – what is all this to me? *I have done my duty*. Undoubtedly, that which puts an end to all other evils cannot be a very great evil itself, and yet it is no easy thing for flesh and blood to despise life. What if death comes? If it does not stay with us, why should we fear it? One hangs himself for a mistress, another leaps the garret window to avoid a choleric master, a third runs away and stabs himself rather than he will be brought back again. We see the force even of our infirmities, and shall we not then do greater things for the love of virtue? To suffer death is but the law of Nature, and it is a great comfort that it can be done but once; in the very convulsions of it we have this consolation, that our pain is near an end, and that it frees us from all the miseries of life. What it is we know not, and it were rash to condemn what we do not understand. But this we presume, either that we shall pass out of this into a better life, where we shall live with tranquillity and splendour in diviner mansions, or else return to our first principles, free from the sense of any inconvenience. There is nothing immortal, nor many things lasting; but by divers ways everything comes to an end. What an arrogance is it then, when the world itself stands condemned to a dissolution, that man alone should expect to live forever? It is unjust not to allow unto the giver the power of disposing of his own bounty, and a folly only to value the present. Death is as much a debt as money, and life is but a journey towards it. Some dispatch it sooner, others later, but we must all have the same period. The thunderbolt is undoubtedly just, that draws, even from those that are struck with it, a veneration. A great soul takes no delight in staying with the body; it considers whence it came, and knows whither it is to go. The day will come that shall separate this mixture of soul and body, of divine and human. My body I will leave where I found it; my soul I will restore to heaven, which would have been there already, but for the clog that keeps it down. And beside, how many men have been the worse for longer living, that might have died with reputation if they had been sooner taken away? How many disappointments of hopeful youths, that have proved dissolute men? Over and above the ruins, shipwrecks, torments, prisons that attend long life: a blessing so deceitful, that if a child were in condition to judge of it, and at liberty to refuse it, he would not take it.

WHAT Providence has made necessary, human prudence should comply with cheerfully: as there is a necessity of death, so that necessity is equal and invincible. No man has cause of complaint for *What God has made necessary, man should comply with cheerfully* that which every man must suffer as well as himself. When we *should* die we *will not*, and when we *would not*, we *must*: but our fate is fixed, and unavoidable is the decree. Why do we then stand trembling when the time comes? Why do we not as well lament that we did not live a thousand years ago, as that we shall not live a thousand years hence? It is but travelling the Great Road, and to the place whither we must all go at last. It is but submitting to the law of Nature, and to that lot which the whole world has suffered, that is gone before us; and so must they too, that are to come after us. Nay, how many thousands, when our time comes, will expire in the same moment with us? He that will not follow shall be drawn by force. And is it not much better now to do that willingly, which we shall otherwise be made to do in spite of our hearts? The sons of mortal parents must expect a mortal posterity; death is the end of great and small. We are born helpless, and exposed to the injuries of all creatures, and of all weathers. The very necessaries of life are deadly to us. We meet with our fate in our dishes, in our cups, and in the very air we breathe; nay, our very birth is inauspicious, for we came into the world weeping, and in the middle of our designs, while we are meditating great matters and stretching of our thoughts to after-ages, death cuts us off, and our longest date is only the revolution of a few years. One man dies at the table, another goes away in his sleep, a third in his mistress's arms, a fourth is stabbed, another is stung with an adder, or crushed with the fall of a house. We have several ways to our end, but the end itself, which is death, is still the same. Whether we die by a sword, by a halter, by a potion, or by a disease, it is all but *death*. A child dies in the swaddling clouts, and an old man at a hundred; they are both mortal alike, though the one goes sooner than the other. All that lies betwixt the cradle and the grave is uncertain. If we compute the *troubles*, the life even of a child is long; if the *sweetness* of the *passage*, that of an old man is short. The whole is slippery and deceitful, and only death certain; and yet all people complain of that which never deceived any man. *Senecio* raised himself from a small beginning to a vast fortune, being very well skilled in the faculties both of getting and of keeping, and either of them was sufficient for the doing of his business. He was a man infinitely careful, both of his patrimony and of his body. He gave me a morning visit (says our author), and after that visit he went away, and spent the rest of the day with a friend of his that was desperately sick. At night he was merry at supper, and seized immediately after with a quinsy, which dispatched him in a few hours. This man that had money at use in all places, and in the very course and height of his prosperity, was thus cut off. How foolish a thing is it then for a man to flatter himself with long hopes, and to pretend to dispose of the future? Nay, the very present slips through our fingers, and there is not that moment which we can call our own. How vain a thing is it for us to enter upon projects, and to say to ourselves, *Well, I will go build, purchase, discharge such offices, settle my affairs, and then retire.* We are all of us born to the same casualties, all equally frail and uncertain of tomorrow. At the very altar, where we pray for life, we learn to die, by seeing the sacrifices killed before us. But there is no need of a wound, or searching the heart for it, when the noose of a cord, or the smothering of a pillow, will do the work. All things have their seasons; they begin, they increase, and they die. The heavens and the earth grow old, and are appointed their periods. That which we call death is but a pause or suspension, and in truth a progress to life; only our thoughts look downward upon the body, and not forward upon things to come. All things under the sun are mortal; cities, empires: and the time will come when it shall be a question where they were, and perchance whether ever they had a being or no. Some will be destroyed by war, others by luxury, fire, inundations, earthquakes. Why should it trouble me then to die, as a forerunner of a universal dissolution? A great mind submits itself to God, and suffers willingly what the law of the universe will otherwise bring to pass upon necessity. That good old man *Bassus* (though with one foot in the grave), how cheerful a mind does he bear? He lives in the view of death, and contemplates his own end with less concern of thought or countenance than he would do another man's. It is a hard lesson, and we are a long time learning it, to receive our death without trouble, especially in the case of *Bassus*. In other deaths there is a mixture of hope; a disease may be cured, a fire quenched, a falling house either propped or avoided; the sea may swallow a man, and throw him up again. A pardon may interpose betwixt the axe and the body, but in the case of old age there is no place for either hope or intercession. Let us live in our bodies therefore, as if we were only to lodge in them this night, and to leave them tomorrow. It is the frequent thought of death that must fortify us against the necessity of it. He that has armed himself against poverty, may perhaps come to live in plenty. A man may strengthen himself against pain, and yet live in a state of health; against the loss of friends, and never lose any. But he that fortifies himself against the fear of death shall most certainly have occasion to employ that virtue. It is the care of a wise and good man to look to his manners and actions, and rather how well he lives, than how long. For to die sooner or later is not the business, but to die well or ill, for *death brings us to immortality*.

CHAPTER 23

AGAINST IMMODERATE SORROW
FOR THE DEATH OF FRIENDS

NEXT to the encounter of death in our own bodies, the most sensible calamity to an honest man is the death of a friend; and we are not in truth without some generous instances of those that have preferred a friend's life before their own; and yet this affliction, which by nature is so grievous to us, is, by virtue and providence, made familiar and easy.

TO lament the death of a friend is both natural and

Sorrow with- just. A sigh or a tear I would allow to his
in bounds is memory, but no profuse or obstinate sor-
allowable row. Clamorous and public lamentations

are not so much the effects of grief, as of vainglory. He that is sadder in company than alone, shows rather the ambition of his sorrow than the piety of it. Nay, and in the violence of his passion, there fall out twenty things that set him a-laughing. At the long run, time cures all, but it were better done by moderation and wisdom. Some people do as good as set a watch upon themselves, as if they were afraid that their grief would make an escape. The ostentation of grief is many times more than the grief itself. When anybody is within hearing, what groans and outcries! When they are alone and private, all is hush and quiet: but as soon as anybody comes in, they are at it again, and down they throw themselves upon the bed, fall to wringing of their hands and wishing of themselves dead, which they might have executed by themselves, but their sorrow goes off with the company. We forsake Nature and run over to the practices of the people that never were the authors of anything that is good. If destiny were to be wrought upon by tears, I would allow you to spend your days and nights in sadness and mourning, tearing of your hair and beating of your breast; but if fate be inexorable, and death will keep what he has taken, grief is to no purpose. And yet I would not advise insensibility and hardness; it were inhumanity, and not virtue, not to be moved at the separation of familiar friends and relations. Now, in such cases, we cannot command ourselves; we cannot forbear weeping, and we ought not to forbear: but let us not pass the bounds of affection, and run into imitation; within these limits it is some ease to the mind.

A wise man gives way to tears in some cases, and cannot avoid them in others, when one is struck with the surprise of ill news, as the death of a friend or the like; or upon the last embrace of an acquaintance *Sorrow is in some cases allowable, and inevitable in others* under the hand of an executioner, he lies under a natural necessity of weeping and trembling. In another case we may indulge our sorrow, as upon the memory of a dead friend's conversation, or kindness, one may let fall tears of generosity and joy. We favour the one, and we are overcome with the other, and this is well: but we are not upon any terms to force them; they may flow of their own accord, without derogating from the dignity of a wise man, who at the same time both preserves his gravity and obeys Nature. Nay, there is a certain *decorum* even in weeping, for excess of sorrow is as foolish as profuse laughter. Why do we not as well cry, when our trees that we took pleasure in shed their leaves, as at the loss of other satisfactions, when the next season repairs them, either with the same again, or others in their places. We may *accuse* fate, but we cannot *alter* it, for it is hard and inexorable, and not to be removed, either with reproaches or tears. They may carry *us* to the *dead*, but never bring *them* back again to us. If reason does not put an end to our sorrows, fortune never will: one is pinched with poverty, another solicited with ambition, and fears the very wealth that he coveted. One is troubled for the loss of children, another for the want of them, so that we shall sooner want tears than matter for them; let us therefore spare that for which we have so much occasion. I do confess that in the very parting of friends there is something of an uneasiness and trouble, but it is rather voluntary than natural, and it is custom more than sense that affects us: we do rather impose a sorrow upon ourselves than submit to it; as people cry when they have company, and when nobody looks on, all is well again. To mourn without measure is folly, and not to mourn at all is insensibility. The best temper is betwixt piety and reason; to be sensible, but neither transported nor cast down. He that can put a stop to his tears and pleasures when he will, is safe. It is an equal infelicity to be either too soft or too hard. We are overcome by the one, and we are put to struggle with the other. There is a certain intemperance in that

sorrow that passes the rules of modesty, and yet great
piety is in many cases a dispensation to good manners.
The loss of a son, or of a friend, cuts a man to the
heart, and there is no opposing the first violence of this
passion; but when a man comes once to deliver himself
wholly up to lamentations, he is to understand, that
though some tears deserve compassion, others are yet
ridiculous. A grief that is fresh finds pity and comfort;
but when it is inveterate it is laughed at, for it is either
counterfeit or foolish. Beside that, to weep excessively
for the dead is an affront to the living. The most justi-
fiable cause of mourning is to see good men come to ill
ends, and virtue oppressed by the iniquity of fortune.
But in this case too, they either suffer resolutely, and
yield us delight in their courage and example, or
meanly, and so give us the less trouble for the loss. He
that dies cheerfully dries up my tears, and he that dies
whiningly does not deserve them. I would bear the
death of friends and children with the same constancy
that I would expect my own, and no more lament the
one than fear the other. He that bethinks himself how
often friends have been parted, will find more time
lost among the living than upon the dead; and the
most desperate mourners are they that cared least for
their friends when they were living, for they think to
redeem their credits for want of kindness to the living
by extravagant ravings after the dead. Some (I know)
will have grief to be only the perverse delight of a restless mind, and sorrows and pleasure to be near akin;
and there are, I am confident, some that find joy even
in their tears. But which is more barbarous, to be

insensible of grief for the death of a friend, or to fish for pleasure in grief, when a son perhaps is burning, or a friend expiring? To forget one's friend, to bury the memory with the body, to lament out of measure, is all inhuman. He that is gone, either would not have his friend tormented, or does not know that he is so: if he does not feel it, it is superfluous; if he does, it is unacceptable to him. If reason cannot prevail, reputation may, for immoderate mourning lessens a man's character. It is a shameful thing for a wise man to make the *weariness* of grieving the *remedy* of it. In time, the most stubborn grief will leave us, if in prudence we do not leave that first.

BUT do I grieve for my friend's sake, or for my own? Why should I afflict myself for the loss of him that is either happy, or not at all in being? In the one case it is envy, and in the other it is madness. We are apt to say, *What would I give to see him again, and to enjoy his conversation! I was never sad in his company; my heart leaped whenever I met him: I want him wherever I go.* All that is to be said is, *The greater the loss, the greater is the virtue to overcome it.* If grieving will do no good, it is an idle thing to grieve; and if that which has befallen one man remains to all, it is as unjust to complain. The whole world is upon the march towards the same point. Why do we not cry for ourselves that are to follow, as well as for him that is gone first? Why do we not as well lament beforehand for that which we know will be, and cannot possibly but be? He is not *gone*, but *sent before.* As there are many things that he has lost, so there

We grieve more for our own sakes than for our friends

are many things that he does not fear: as anger, jeal-
ousy, envy, &c. Is he not more happy in desiring nothing, than miserable in what he has lost? We do not
mourn for the absent, why then for the dead, who are
effectually no other? We have lost one blessing, but we
have many left; and shall not all these satisfactions support us against one sorrow?

THE comfort of having a friend may be taken
away, but not that of having had one. As
there is a sharpness in some fruits, and a
bitterness in some wines that please us,
so there is a mixture in the remembrance
*A friend may be
taken away, but
not the comfort
of friendship*
of friends, where the loss of the company is sweetened
again by the contemplation of their virtues. In some
respects I have lost what I had, and in others I retain
still what I have lost. It is an ill construction of Providence to reflect only upon my friend's being taken
away without any regard to the benefit of his being
once given me. Let us therefore make the best of our
friends while we have them, for how long we shall
keep them is uncertain. I have lost a hopeful son, but
how many fathers have been deceived in their expecta-
tions? And many noble families have been destroyed
by luxury and riot? He that grieves for the loss of a
son, what if he had lost a friend? And yet he that has
lost a friend has more cause of joy that he once had
him, than of grief that he is taken away. Shall a man
bury his friendship with his friend? We are ungrateful
for that which is past, in hope of what is to come; as if
that which is to come would not quickly be past too.
That which is past we are sure of. We may receive

satisfaction, it is true, both from the future and what is already past, the one by expectation and the other by memory; only the one may possibly not come to pass, and it is impossible to make the other not to have been.

BUT there is no applying of consolation to fresh and bleeding sorrow; the very discourse irritates the grief and inflames it. It is like an unseasonable medicine in a disease; when the first violence is over, it will be more tractable, and endure the handling. Those people whose minds are weakened by long felicity, may be allowed to groan and complain, but it is otherwise with those that have led their days in misfortunes. A long course of adversity has this good in it, that though it vexes a body a great while, it comes to harden us at last — as a raw soldier shrinks at every wound and dreads the surgeon more than an enemy, whereas the *veteran* sees his own body cut and lamed, with as little concern as if it were another's. With the same resolution should we stand the shock and cure of all misfortunes; we are never the better for our experience if we have not yet learned to be miserable. And there is no thought of curing us by the diversion of sports and entertainments; we are apt to fall into relapses, wherefore we had better overcome our sorrow than delude it.

There is no dealing with the first transports of sorrow

CHAPTER 24

CONSOLATIONS AGAINST
BANISHMENT AND BODILY PAIN

I T is a masterpiece to draw good out of evil, and by the help of virtue to improve misfortunes into blessings. *It is a sad condition*, you will say, *for a man to be barred the freedom of his own country*. And is not this the case of thousands that we meet every day in the streets? Some for ambition, others to negotiate, or for curiosity, delight, friendship, study, experience, luxury, vanity, discontent; some to exercise their virtues, others their vices, and not a few to prostitute either their bodies or their eloquence? To pass now from pleasant countries into the worst of islands, let them be never so barren or rocky, the people never so barbarous, or the clime never so intemperate: he that is banished thither shall find many strangers to live there for their pleasure. The mind of man is naturally curious and restless, which is no wonder, considering their divine original, for heavenly things are always in motion: witness the stars and the orbs, which are perpetually moving, rolling, and changing of place, and according to the law and appointment of Nature. But here are no woods, you will say, no rivers, no gold nor pearl, no commodity for traffic or commerce; nay, hardly provision enough to keep the inhabitants from starving. It is very right; here are no palaces, no artificial grottos or materials for luxury and excess, but we lie under the protection of heaven; and a poor cottage

63

for a retreat is more worth than the most magnificent temple when that cottage is consecrated by an honest man under the guard of his virtue. Shall any man think banishment grievous when he may take such company along with him? Nor is there any banishment but yields enough for our necessities, and no kingdom is sufficient for superfluities. It is the mind that makes us rich in a desert, and if the body be but kept alive, the soul enjoys all spiritual felicities in abundance. What signifies the being banished from one spot of ground to another to a man that has his thoughts above, and can look forward and backward, and wherever he pleases, and that wherever he is, has the same matter to work upon? The body is but the prison, or the clog of the mind, subjected to punishments, robberies, diseases; but the mind is sacred and spiritual, and liable to no violence. Is it that a man shall want garments or covering in banishment? The body is as easily clothed as fed, and Nature has made nothing hard that is necessary. But if nothing will serve us but rich embroideries and scarlet, it is none of fortune's fault that we are poor, but our own. Nay, suppose a man should have all restored him back again that he has lost, it will come to nothing, for he will want more after that, to satisfy his desires, than he did before to supply his necessities. Insatiable appetites are not so much a thirst, as a disease.

TO come lower now: where is that people, or nation, that have not changed their place of abode? Some by the fate of war; others have been cast by tempests, shipwrecks, or want of provisions upon unknown coasts. Some have been forced abroad by pestilence, sedition, earthquakes, surcharge of people at home. Some travel to see the world, others for commerce, but, in fine, it is clear that

Banishment is but change of place; in which sense, all people and nations have been banished

upon some reason or other, the whole race of mankind have shifted their quarters, changed their very names, as well as their habitations, insomuch that we have lost the very memorials of what they were. All these transportations of people, what are they, but public banishments? The very *founder* of the *Roman Empire* was an *exile*. Briefly, the whole world has been transplanted, and one mutation treads upon the heel of another. That which one man desires turns another man's stomach, and he that proscribes me today shall himself be cast out tomorrow. We have however this comfort in our misfortune: we have the same nature, the same Providence, and we carry our virtues along with us. And this blessing we owe to the Almighty Power, call it what you will, either a *God* or an *Incorporeal Reason*, a *Divine Spirit*, or *Fate*, and the *unchangeable course of causes and effects*: it is, however, so ordered that nothing can be taken from us but what we can well spare, and that which is most magnificent and valuable continues with us. Wherever we go, we have the heavens over our heads and no farther from us than they were before, and so long as we can entertain our eyes and thoughts with those glories, what matter is it what ground we tread upon?

IN the case of pain or sickness, it is only the body that is affected. It may take off the speed of a footman,

Pain only affects or bind the hands of a cobbler, but the
the body, not the mind is still at liberty to hear, learn,
mind teach, advise, and to do other good offices. It is an example of public benefit, a man that is in
pain and patient. Virtue may show itself as well in the
bed as in the field, and he that cheerfully encounters
the terrors of death and corporal anguish is as great a
man as he that most generously hazards himself in a
battle. A disease, it is true, bars us of some pleasures,
but procures others. Drink is never so grateful to us as
in a burning fever, nor meat as when we have fasted
ourselves sharp and hungry. The patient may be for-
bidden some sensual satisfaction, but no physician will
forbid us the delight of the mind. Shall we call any sick
man miserable because he must give over his intemperance of wine and gluttony, and betake himself to a
diet of more sobriety and less expense, and abandon
his luxury, which is the distemper of the mind as well
as of the body? It is troublesome, I know, at first to
abstain from the pleasures we have been used to, and
to endure hunger and thirst; but in a little time we lose
the very appetite, and it is no trouble then to be without that which we do not desire. In diseases there are
great pains; but if they be long, they remit and give us
some intervals of ease; if short and violent, either they
dispatch *us* or consume *themselves*: so that either their
respites make them tolerable, or the extremity makes
them short. So merciful is God Almighty to us that
our torments cannot be very sharp and lasting. The
acutest pains are those that affect the nerves, but there
is this comfort in them too, that they will quickly

make us stupid and insensible. In cases of extremity, let us call to mind the most eminent instances of patience and courage, and turn our thoughts from our afflictions to the contemplation of virtue. Suppose it be the stone, the gout, nay, the rack itself: how many have endured it without so much as a groan, or a word speaking; without so much as asking for relief, or giving an answer to a question? Nay, they have laughed at the tormentors upon the very torture, and provoked them to new experiments of their cruelty, which they have had still in derision. The *asthma* I look upon as of all diseases the most importune; the physicians call it *the meditation of death*, as being rather an agony than a sickness: the fit holds not above an hour, as nobody is long in expiring. There are three things grievous in sickness: the fear of death, bodily pain, and the intermission of our pleasures. The first is to be imputed to Nature, not to the disease, for we do not die because we are sick, but because we live. Nay, sickness itself has preserved many a man from dying.

CHAPTER 25

POVERTY TO A WISE MAN IS RATHER A BLESSING THAN A MISFORTUNE

NO man shall ever be poor, that goes to himself for what he wants, and that is the readiest way to riches. Nature indeed will have her due, but yet whatsoever is beyond necessity is precarious, and not necessary. It is not her business to gratify the palate, but to satisfy a craving stomach: bread, when a man is hungry, does his work, let it be never so coarse; and water when he is a-dry; let his thirst be quenched and Nature is satisfied, no matter whence it comes or whether he drinks in gold, silver, or in the hollow of his hand. To promise a man riches and to teach him poverty, is to deceive him: but shall I call him poor that wants nothing, though he may be beholden for it to his patience rather than to his fortune? Or shall any man deny him to be rich, whose riches can never be taken away? Whether is it better to have much, or enough? He that has much desires more, which shows that he has not yet enough; but he that has enough is at rest. Shall a man be reputed the less rich for not having that for which he shall be banished, for which his very wife or son shall poison him, that which gives him security in war and quiet in peace, which he possesses without danger, and disposes of without trouble? No man can be poor that has enough, nor rich that covets more than he has. *Alexan-*

der, after all his conquests, complained that he wanted more worlds; he desired something more, even when he had gotten all: and that which was sufficient for human nature was not enough for one man. Money never made any man rich, for the more he had, the more he still coveted. The richest man that ever lived is poor in my opinion, and in any man's may be so: but he that keeps himself to the stint of Nature, does neither feel poverty, nor fear it; nay, even in poverty itself there are some things superfluous. Those which the world calls happy, their felicity is a false splendour that dazzles the eyes of the vulgar, but our rich man is glorious and happy within. There is no ambition in hunger, or thirst: let there be food, and no matter for the table, the dish, and the servants, nor with what meats Nature is satisfied. Those are the torments of luxury, that rather stuff the stomach than fill it: it studies rather to cause an appetite, than to allay it. It is not for us to say, *this is not handsome, that is common, the other offends my eye.* Nature provides for health, not delicacy. When the trumpet sounds a charge, the poor man knows that he is not aimed at: when they cry out *fire*, his body is all he has to look after; if he be to take a journey, there is no blocking up of streets, and thronging of passages for a parting compliment. A small matter fills his belly and contents his mind; he lives from hand to mouth, without carking or fearing for tomorrow. The temperate rich man is but his counterfeit; his wit is quicker, and his appetite calmer.

NO man finds poverty a trouble to him, but he that thinks it so: and he that thinks it so, makes it so.

Poverty is only troublesome in opinion Does not a rich man travel more at ease, with less luggage and fewer servants? Does he not eat, many times, as little and as coarse in the field, as a poor man? Does he not, for his own pleasure, sometimes and for variety, feed upon the ground, and use only earthen vessels? Is not he a madman then, that always fears what he often desires, and dreads the thing that he takes delights to imitate? He that would know the worst of poverty, let him but compare the looks of the rich and of the poor, and he shall find the poor man to have a smoother brow, and to be more merry at heart; or if any trouble befalls him, it passes over like a cloud: whereas the other, either his good humour is counterfeit, or his melancholy deep and ulcerated, and the worse, because he dares not publicly own his misfortune; but he is forced to play the part of a happy man, even with a cancer in his heart. His felicity is but personated, and if he were but stripped of his ornaments, he would be contemptible. In buying of a horse we take off his clothes and his trappings, and examine his shape and body, for fear of being cozened: and shall we put an estimate upon a man for being set off by his fortune and quality? Nay, if we see anything of ornament about him, we are to suspect him the more for some infirmity under it. He that is not content in poverty would not be so neither in plenty, for the fault is not in the thing, but in the mind. If that be sickly, remove him from a kennel to a palace, he is at the same pass, for he carries his disease along with him. What can be happier than that condition, both of mind and of fortune, from which we cannot fall? What can be a greater felicity than in a covetous designing age, for a man to live safe among informers and thieves? It puts a poor man into the very condition of Providence, that gives all without reserving anything to itself. How happy is he that owes nothing but to himself, and only that which he can easily refuse, or easily pay! I do not reckon him poor that has but a little, but he is so that covets more; it is a fair degree of plenty, to have what is necessary. Whether had a man better find saturity in want, or hunger in plenty? It is not the augmenting of our fortunes, but the abating of our appetites that makes us rich. Why may not a man as well contemn riches in his own coffers as in another mans? And rather hear that they are his, than feel them to be so? Though it is a great matter not to be corrupted, even by having them under the same roof. He is the greater man that is honestly poor in the middle of plenty, but he is the most secure that is free from the temptation of that plenty, and has the least matter for another to design upon. It is no great business for a poor man to preach the contempt of riches, or for a rich man to extol the benefits of poverty, because we do not know how either the one or the other would behave himself in the contrary condition. The best proof is the doing of it by choice, and not by necessity; for the practice of poverty in jest is a preparation toward the bearing of it in earnest. But it is yet a generous disposition so to provide for the worst of fortunes, as what may be easily borne: the premeditation makes them not only tolerable, but delightful to us; for there is that in them, without which nothing can be comfortable, that is to say, security. If there were nothing else in poverty but the certain knowledge of our friends, it were yet a most desirable blessing, when every man leaves us but those that love us. It is a shame to place the happiness of life in gold and silver, for which bread and water is sufficient; or, at the worst, hunger puts an end to hunger. For the honour of *poverty*, it was both the *foundation* and the *cause of the Roman Empire*; and no man was ever yet so poor, but he had enough to carry him to his journey's end.

ALL I desire is that my poverty may not be a bur-*Mediocrity is* den to myself, or make me so to others; *the best state* and that is the best state of fortune, that is *of fortune* neither directly necessitous, nor far from it. A mediocrity of fortune, with a gentleness of mind, will preserve us from fear or envy; which is a desirable condition, for no man wants power to do mischief. We never consider the blessing of coveting nothing, and the glory of being full in ourselves, without depending upon fortune. With parsimony a little is sufficient, and without it nothing, whereas frugality makes a poor man rich. It we lose an estate, we had better never have had it: he that has least to lose, has least to fear; and those are better satisfied whom fortune never favoured, than those whom she has forsaken. The state is most commodious that lies betwixt poverty and plenty. *Diogenes* understood this very well, when he put himself into an incapacity of losing anything. That course of life is most commodious which is both safe and wholesome; the body is to be indulged no farther than for health, and rather mortified than not kept in subjection to the mind. It is necessary to provide against hunger, thirst and cold, and somewhat for a covering to shelter us against other inconveniencies, but not a pin matter whether it be of turf or of marble. A man may lie as warm, and as dry, under a thatched as under a gilded roof. Let the mind be great and glorious, and all other things are despicable in comparison. *The future is uncertain, and I had rather beg of myself not to desire anything, than of fortune to bestow it.*

 THE END

Seneca on Friendship, Death, and Poverty
Roger L'Estrange and Keith Seddon
Published by Lulu 2011
© 2011 Keith Seddon
ISBN 978-1-4710-3581-4 (paperback)

Typeset in Bembo Book by the editor using Microsoft Word 2010.
Proofs checked and reviewed in Portable Document Format
created using open source PDFCreator 1.2.3.

NOTE ON THE TYPEFACE

All text is set in Bembo Book, designed by Robin Nicholas.

'Originally drawn by Monotype in 1929, the Bembo® design was inspired by the types cut by Francesco Griffo and used by Aldus Manutius in 1495 to print Cardinal Bembo's tract *De Aetna*. A beautiful design with tall ascending lowercase and elegant letterforms, Bembo has been a favourite for book setting for over 70 years. ... Considered by many to be one of Stanley Morison's finest achievements during his tenure as Typographical Advisor to the Monotype Corporation, Bembo has consistently been a bestselling typeface, both in its original hot metal form and in today's digital formats. ... This new digital version of Bembo, called Bembo Book, has been designed to be more suited to text setting in the size range from 10 point to 18 point. Based on the hot metal 10/18 point drawings, which were used to cut all sizes from 10 point to 24 point, this new face has been carefully drawn to produce similar results to those achieved from the hot metal version when letterpress printed. The project started in 2002 when a high quality UK printing house asked for a digital version of Bembo which would give a similar appearance on the page to the 13 point hot metal they were currently using. Hot metal drawings were digitised and extensive editing was carried out on the resultant outlines to ensure that design features and overall colour from the digital output remained close to that of the letterpress product. The resultant typeface is slightly narrower than existing digital versions of Bembo, it is a little more economical in use and gives excellent colour to continuous pages of text. Ascending lowercase letters are noticeably taller than capitals, giving an elegant, refined look to the text.'

(Slightly abridged from http://www.monotype.co.uk/bembo/)

Made in the USA
Middletown, DE
11 September 2018